ADELPHI PAPERS

NUMBER ONE HUNDRED AND FIFTY

Soviet Perspectives on Security

by Helmut Sonnenfeldt and William G. Hyland

THE INTERNATIONAL INSTITUTE FOR STRATEGIC STUDIES
18 ADAM STREET LONDON WC2N 6AL

ADELPHI PAPER NO. 150

Helmut Sonnenfeldt is a Guest Scholar, The Brookings In-
stitution, Washington DC, and formerly a US State
Department Counsellor. William G. Hyland was a member
of the National Security Council secretariat and is now a
Senior Fellow, The Georgetown Center for Strategic and
International Studies, Washington DC. Both were closely
involved with Soviet- American relations during the 1960s
and 1970s.

First published Spring 1979

ISBN 0 86079 027 4
ISSN 0567-932X

*The International Institute for Strategic Studies was founded in 1958 as a centre for
the provision of information on and research into the problems of international
security, defence and arms control in the nuclear age. It is international in its Council and staff, and its membership is drawn from over fifty countries. It is independent of governments and is not the advocate of any particular interest.*

*The Institute is concerned with strategic questions – not just with the military
aspects of security but with the social and economic sources and political and moral
implications of the use and existence of armed force: in other words with the basic
problems of peace.*

*The Institute's publications are intended for a much wider audience than its own
membership and are available to the general public on subscription or singly.*

Printed in Great Britain by The Eastern Press Ltd., London and Reading.

CONTENTS

Soviet Perspectives on Security

INTRODUCTION

The purpose of this essay is to explore Soviet conceptions of security. More particularly, we are concerned with determining how successive Soviet leaderships have sought to define the security requirements of the Soviet Union, how they have gone about satisfying these requirements and how successful they have been.

To examine the security conceptions of any nation, or those of its leaders, is at best fraught with difficulties. Security is not a fixed or quantifiable condition, although some of its elements are concrete enough. But it is in many respects a state of mind, which is affected by many stimuli, some going far back into historic experience.

The Soviet case is beset by particular problems because so much of the USSR's own discussion of security issues is either shrouded in secrecy or obscured by ritualistic and convoluted terminology. Soviet conduct is, of course, visible and constitutes a major and important body of evidence. But the motivations behind the conduct, and the debates and judgments associated with it, are rarely elucidated in the documentary material that is only sporadically available. It hardly needs to be noted that there is no investigative reporting in Moscow, nor a Freedom of Information Act, nor any wholesale opening of archives. Thus, even at this late date, we must still rely on speculation about the Soviet role in the invasion of Korea in 1950 or, to take a more recent example, about the calculations, expectations and objectives that led Khrushchev to deploy missiles to Cuba in 1962. For written material, we have to rely almost entirely on the public

record such as official releases, speeches, articles and diplomatic communications.

Publicly available pronouncements cannot, of course, be discounted. They serve, among other things, as one form of communication between the Soviet leadership, the subordinate elites and the population at large. They are also used in some measure to communicate with foreign Communist parties and with the outside world generally. Careful scrutiny of these materials over time can and does provide some insight into Soviet concerns and goals.

Analysis of official or officially inspired Soviet materials has been intensively conducted in the West for more than thirty years now. It has produced a methodology which involves in the main a search for shifts in emphasis or phrasing, frequently minute, which are interpreted to reflect policy changes or differences among the leadership elite. At the same time, most Western analysts believe that the Soviet Union usually means what she says on policy matters and should be taken at her word; that is to say, the reiteration of statements should be accorded substantial weight. We tend to agree with these approaches to the analysis of the contents of public Soviet materials.

But it needs to be remembered constantly that in sifting these materials one is still dealing only with very partial evidence, and that what is withheld almost certainly greatly outweighs in importance what is accessible. Among other things, we are denied the kind of 'feel' that we might gain from an occasional sampling of the papers used by top leaders in their deliberations. It is a lack of which one is particularly conscious when dealing with an issue like security, which involves intangibles.

The absence of what would normally be considered historical evidence has been somewhat offset in recent years by the intensification of contact between Soviet and foreign representatives at summit level and below. Most of these occur in a bargaining context. They lack the candour and, generally speaking, the informality and the broad range of topics which characterize meetings among Western leaders, for example. They do offer a hint, but only a hint, about the preoccupations of Soviet leaders. In addition, Soviet representatives (below decision-making levels on the whole, but members of the governing elite) participate in increasing numbers in exchanges with foreign counterparts. Over the past few years they have adapted their discourse to a terminology and a style more compatible with those of Western debates about the issues that concern us here.

But even the greater intensity and variety of contacts and the decline of jargon leave considerable room for doubt about whether the USSR thinks about security issues in the terms to which we are accustomed in our own deliberations over these issues. In any event, anyone who has participated in discussions with Soviet representatives will be aware that, even if the terms of discussion have become more compatible, differences in substance and perception remain wide and deep.

Thus, the problem of inadequate and defective evidence is compounded by the problem of perspective. Any attempt by foreigners to comprehend and represent the conceptions of other nations and their leaders is always beset by pitfalls; these dangers are almost certainly more pronounced when dealing with the USSR.

Relations with the USSR have been a matter of enormous concern for Americans and many others for more than a generation. Issues are involved which have the gravest and most far-reaching implications. Almost inevitably in such circumstances, the line between analysis and policy preferences becomes quite fine. Indeed, experience has demonstrated that certain analytical conclusions are not merely a contribution to scholarship or theory; they may well become the basis for action. To call on an example from the past, one needs only to read some of the official American documents now available for the 1949–50 period to see the close connection between conclusions reached about the nature of the Soviet Union and her objectives on the one hand, and the policy options considered and advocated on the other.

We recognize, therefore, that we cannot be fully objective in the pages that follow. Inevitably, we will be presenting something of our own view of Soviet perspectives, based on evidence with the imperfections we have noted.

Our discussion seeks to focus on Soviet security perspectives. But security is, in part, a function of power, although the correlation is far from a simple one. Many a nation lacking some of the principal prerequisites of power nevertheless feels relatively secure against external attack or pressure. Other more powerful nations may be, and often are, troubled by anxieties concerning their survival or freedom of action. Some states seek to curb their fears by accumulating military power; others rely on alliances as well, on skilful diplomacy, on the manipulation of their putative adversaries and on many other devices and courses. For the USSR, power – especially its military component – has long been considered the principal means of assuring survival and the creation of conditions in which the regime can pursue its domestic and other aims. Consequently, in undertaking this examination of the Soviet view and pursuit of security, we will constantly encounter the question of Soviet power and its role and purposes. But we will also encounter the complexities of the interaction between security and power, particularly as, for the USSR, concepts like alliances, interdependence and international institution-building have until now played a far less significant role in the search for security than has been true for most Western nations.

At the conclusion of the essay we will also have something to say on the role of disarmament and arms control in the Soviet perspective on security. Disarmament (arms control is still a relatively rare term in Soviet parlance) has always been prominent in Soviet propaganda and diplomacy. It has served various purposes since the founding of the Soviet Union, including the promotion of security, although its centrality in this respect is questionable.

The approach we have used in our discussion is basically chronological. That is, viewing

Soviet conduct as a whole, we will trace the evolution of Soviet security conceptions through various stages from the Revolution to the present. The essay is organized roughly around the leadership periods of Lenin, Stalin, Khrushchev and Brezhnev. We recognize, of course, that changes in Soviet leadership are not necessarily coterminous with historical periods, especially when the problem under study is partly affected by developments and events that are either not at all, or only very indirectly, under Soviet control. Still, we have found this rough division of the period under consideration useful for our purposes, acknowledging that the stages in the evolution we are seeking to trace are not wholly congruent with the tenures of the four men who have ruled the USSR since 1917.

I. THE REVOLUTIONARY PERSPECTIVE

There has been a tendency in Western analysis to regard Soviet 'goals' as immutable and to interpret changes in policy and fluctuations in the tone and climate of East–West relations as essentially 'tactical' shifts. This is far from a unanimous Western view, but it is widely and tenaciously held. It is encouraged by the USSR herself because of her constant insistence that she is operating on the basis of 'scientific' doctrines or even laws (which the USSR herself 'discovers' and interprets); that she is the agent of history, which is said to be on her side; and that, while policies are adapted to new and changing conditions, the commitment of Soviet policy to 'Leninist' prescriptions remains unwavering. There is a large body of Soviet pronouncements that holds strategy to be broadly unchanging while allowing for – indeed, urging – shifts in tactics as required by prevailing circumstances.

One consequence is that analysts speculate endlessly about where tactics end and strategy begins. Similarly, the somewhat contrary point is often made that when 'tactics' are infinitely flexible, they are bound sooner or later to affect even the most devoutly held goals; resolution of these conflicting views is unlikely to be accomplished by abstract argument.

Turning to the problem of security, then, it can readily be seen that the quest for it has been among the most basic and persistent Soviet concerns since the Revolution. Survival is the most fundamental task of any state, and hence of the governments of all states. It is also the most basic element in any concept of security. Very soon after the Revolution the Bolshevik state began to manifest a degree of concern about its survival not dissimilar to that of other states or of its Tsarist predecessor.

Indeed, at the outset the new Soviet government could not ignore this most elementary aspect of security: a large part of the Soviet Union was occupied by the German army, Bolshevik authority was tenuous, and war or peace was an urgent political question in 1917. What constituted the most effective means of securing Soviet power was an urgent, practical problem and no longer a theoretical proposition to be debated by exiles in the coffee houses of Zurich. Soviet pronouncements insist that Lenin set the fundamental course even then, and that Soviet policy has simply been elaborated in the light of modern conditions.

Yet it seems obvious that the question of what constitutes security has been answered differently at various times in the history of the Soviet Union. And, despite the generally high degree of uniformity of Soviet pronouncements on matters of high policy, it has been answered differently by different Soviet leaders.

In the early days of the Revolution, and for many years before it occurred, most Bolsheviks appeared to be genuinely convinced that after the Revolution had taken place in Russia, similar upheavals in adjacent countries would quickly follow. Communist theory, in fact, had assumed that more advanced 'capitalist' countries would have their revolutions well before backward Russia. In the event, it was believed that Russia and her ruling proletariat would soon find themselves surrounded by class allies who had wrested power from the bourgeoisie; frontiers and state sovereignty would lose their meaning, and class solidarity would override national differences as old political entities became caught up in revolutionary change. The security problem would thus no longer present itself in its traditional form.

3

These early notions constituted perhaps the most radical departure from the conventional conception of security which had evolved historically in the system of states and nations that had developed since the Middle Ages. The Bolsheviks did not see themselves at first as governing a state but as leading a revolutionary detachment, part of a movement which, if not world-wide, would be widespread, at least in Europe. Security to them meant the physical survival and the further development of the regime that had been established in a part of Russia; it was an important but nevertheless temporary problem. It also meant safeguarding the regime's ability to institute the societal and other changes it planned – but still in the context of a broader, revolutionary environment. The content of these notions of survival and development did not in themselves differ significantly from those entertained by rulers of traditional states. What was new was the conception that survival and the fulfilment of revolutionary goals depended on similar events occurring in adjacent and other countries, and the conviction that these events would then merge into a single universal movement.

Since the survival of the Russian Revolution and the implementation of its goals were seen as depending on revolutions elsewhere, it was only natural that the Russian revolutionary vanguard should seek to trigger such revolutions and help to sustain them. Thus, security clearly was not confined within the old frontiers of Russia, nor within the areas where the Russian revolutionaries held sway (which were far smaller than the territory of Russia, however defined at that fluid moment); it became consciously and deliberately contingent on events well beyond those territorial confines. Yet the capacity of the Russian revolutionaries to affect events beyond the borders of the Soviet Union, and even within their own area of more or less tenuous control, was highly circumscribed. They did have certain ties with revolutionaries elsewhere, but their principal instruments were the presumed force of their ideas and doctrines, and the illusion that history had ordained a revolutionary tide in the capitalist world at that particular moment. These notions, however, proved to be false, and the more clearly their falsity was demonstrated, the more the Bolsheviks, lacking at that time other, tradi-

tional manifestations of power, resorted to conspiratorial, clandestine and other means of encouraging revolutionary movements.

Events unfolded quite differently from expectations. Soviet-style revolutions were confined to a very few countries and proved to be short-lived. Circumstances in the Soviet Union, and the manner in which Lenin's Bolsheviks staged the take-over of the country's government and other institutions, proved to be virtually unique. The USSR soon found herself confronting problems typical of those encountered by states functioning within a system of states. Having challenged the outside world with revolutionary upheaval, she now had to cope with numerous threats to her own territorial integrity and to the survival of the new regime. While in many countries, adjacent as well as more distant, there sprang up Communist parties and other groups sympathetic to the Soviet state, these turned out to have only a limited capacity to support the Soviet rulers' quest to secure themselves against external threats. Their capacity to buttress the new regime in its struggles against internal enemies was even more limited. The novel notions of security and how to promote it entertained by the Russian Bolsheviks thus had only a very brief life, although they continued to colour the security conceptions that subsequently evolved.

The Communist rulers of the USSR had to adjust to the fact that their earlier definitions of the conditions for survival and of how to ensure it were no longer pertinent, and may indeed have been no more than hopes in the first place. But they were convinced that if the country and the hope of eventual widespread revolution were to survive, the regime itself had to be preserved. To Soviet leaders, and to the evolving elite with which they surrounded themselves, national security (to use a Western term) became synonymous with regime security.

These re-definitions of security, which began in Lenin's lifetime, did not come easily. Many of the early disputes and schisms in the regime revolved precisely around the ability of the new revolutionary state to survive. Even before Lenin's death important sections of the revolutionary leadership remained persuaded that the Soviet Union and her regime could not long survive as an island in a capitalist sea. They were dubious about, and opposed to, Lenin's domestic concessions, as in the case of the New Economic Plan, by which he sought to safeguard the economic viability of the Soviet Union. Some also doubted the wisdom and propriety of Lenin's willingness to deal with capitalist powers in the early 1920s in an effort to prevent the formation of hostile coalitions against the Soviet state. Hence the alternative policy associated broadly with Trotsky, that of permanent revolution and active support for revolutionary movements and enterprises in other countries, continued to enjoy support.

Stalin's victory established an enduring conception of security that in its fundamental elements was essentially traditional. The Soviet Union was a state which had to stand guard over her frontiers and territorial integrity. To do so, she needed military forces to deter or ward off potential invaders; she could utilize – and even to an extent rely upon – the admittedly fragile but still not insignificant protection of the 'bourgeois' international order and its legal norms; she could seek alliances or other forms of association, including economic ones, with other members of the traditional state system; and she could and would try to manipulate the external balance of power. Before turning to this new period and the evolution of more traditional security policy, it is worth noting some of the effects of this early period on both the Soviet Union and her adversaries.

First, the Communist International absorbed much of the energy of the Soviet regime and in a sense supplanted more normal forms of diplomacy. Since the Soviet Union was excluded from the European councils, her reliance on foreign Communists was in part a natural reaction, but it may be that the alliance gave the Soviet regime a false impression of the ability of foreign Communists to influence events. In any case, the maintenance of Party links with Moscow were a constant source of suspicion abroad and continued to play a role in the exclusion of the Soviet regime from European affairs.

Second, the question of the 'legitimacy' of the Soviet regime lingered on for a considerable period. The Soviet Union herself contributed to the notion that what was happening in the USSR was transitory and bound to be replaced by some new revolutionary order in Europe. The regime's opponents abroad also continued to hope and believe (though for different reasons) that it would not last. There was widespread expectation that some upheaval would take place or, if not, that the regime's character would evolve in a more benign and traditional direction.

Thus, in the post-Lenin period the regime found itself having to define its own interests, and being forced to do so in a climate still essentially hostile, if not overtly threatening.

II. CONSOLIDATION AND NEW DANGER

Traditional conceptions of security – and far from revolutionary methods of safeguarding it – continued to be accompanied by other elements that gave Soviet views of security a special character. Even as Stalin established the most rigid and repressive internal order and created the first modern totalitarian state, he believed in and practised a form of forward defence deriving from the Bolshevik notion that class solidarity extended beyond national frontiers. Particularly when the external dangers to her security mounted in the mid-1930s, through the consolidation of the Nazi regime in Germany, the Soviet Union sought to build 'reserves' among Communist parties and sympathizers abroad to consolidate her own strength. She gradually ended the sectarian phase of the external Communist parties, ordering and pressing them to seek allies among non-Communist parties and other groups so as to form united fronts against the Fascist threat.

It is quite possible that Stalin saw these alliances as temporary arrangements dictated by the Nazi threat and that, in some instances at least, he envisaged subsequent stages when Communist take-overs could be staged (for example, in Spain). In other words, the Soviet conception of security, while heavily conditioned by anxieties about external dangers (as well as internal threats from residual 'capitalist' elements), retained offensive aspects harking back to earlier notions of spreading Communist revolutions and class alliances transcending national borders. Pretensions to the leadership of the international working class were muted but not renounced. This was the united-front tactic, in fact, built on the mechanisms of the Comintern which had its origins in the early revolutionary optimism that had prevailed immediately after the Revolution. And, under Soviet orders, Communists sought to retain their separate identity to avoid contamination by other groups and theories.

Still, for the time being at least, such offensive aspects were subordinated to more immediate concerns: the search for allies wherever they could be found, including alliances formed through a 'collective security' system; and the effort to deter and delay external aggression and prevent the isolation of the USSR in the event of such aggression.

In the end, these concerns led to an alliance with the enemy himself, when it appeared that neither united fronts nor alliance arrangements could be worked out with the Western democracies and with Germany's potential victims in Eastern and South-eastern Europe. (The Western democracies and their Polish and Romanian associates may have been short-sighted in their failure to enter into defence arrangements with the USSR – most historians believe this to be the case. But it is worth reflecting that it was not the first time, and certainly not the last, that the Soviet Union's own conduct and the legacy of her revolutionary pretensions served to heighten the dangers to her own security and prevent co-operative measures that might have reduced them.)

The Nazi–Soviet alliance quintessentially represented the use of a traditional means of seeking safety or of delaying danger – the manipulation of external forces. But, cynicism (or realism) apart, it was another instance, and perhaps the most dramatic up to that time, of a recognition that the imperatives of security required certain entanglements with the external world of class enemies. Moreover, as the period between 1939 and 1941 was to show, in Soviet eyes the interests of security even required the propitiation of the potential enemy with economic and military support while class allies were left to their own devices – and in consequence deserted the socialist motherland in droves. In addition, as had been evident on earlier occasions after the Revolution, security considerations were seen as ample justification for the acquisition of territory and demands for spheres of influence and control (as advanced in Soviet–Nazi diplomatic haggling in 1940), with no regard for 'revolutionary' conditions or the interests and concerns of indigenous Communist parties.

Thus, in the twenty years after the consolidation of Soviet power, the regime's security conception had evolved from considerations determined largely by the expectations of Communist revolutionary doctrines to ones quite similar to those that had traditionally assured the physical survival of nation-states in times of peril. Since they had not envisaged a single Communist state, Communist doctrines appeared to have little to offer to meet these concerns in practical terms, although they were used to consolidate further Stalin's domestic power. Externally, the Soviet Union was concerned with her essential territorial integrity and physical security; she sought to extend her frontiers as far as possible against the incursions of the potential enemy; she sought allies, regardless of political orientation; she tried to buy time with economic and other concessions; and she set aside revolutionary goals abroad both because they obstructed the palliation of more fundamental anxieties about survival and because, if pursued, they might even have heightened the threat.

It may be said that at this moment of grave danger and considerable weakness the Soviet definition of security involved the most elementary imperative of survival and little else. When the dangers confronting the regime became even graver after the Nazi invasion, it did not, in seeking to assure its survival, shrink from moderating certain of the internal essentials of Communist rule by invoking, *inter alia*, nationalism, patriotism, military discipline and prestige, faith and religion to motivate and mobilize the population against the external threat. The survival of the country and the survival of the leadership were still essentially synonymous, but a certain dilution of the character of the regime occurred which, in conjunction with but quite separately from the external threat, might in fact have placed its survival in question, had the Soviet Union not succeeded in reversing her military fortunes.

The point here is not just that Stalin proved extremely flexible and cynical in pursuing his goals; it is somewhat simpler but no less important: Soviet conceptions of fundamental interests and of how to protect and advance them have not been immutable. The means chosen by, or forced upon, the regime in the pursuit of its interests have involved not only choices normally described as tactical or expedient, but also some that could not have been readily derived from the basic Marxist–Leninist texts or even from the statements of the very practitioners of the policies outlined above. The Soviet conception of security, and the actions designed to safeguard it, must then be seen in the light as much of Soviet operational conduct as of Soviet pronouncements and the Marxist–Leninist classics. Predispositions stemming from the Bolshevik heritage of the leadership can be and have been significantly affected by other factors.

World War II and After

World War II – still referred to, characteristically, as the Great Patriotic War – was plainly a deeply traumatic experience for the Soviet Union. Not only did it cause enormous destruction and human suffering, but it shook the regime to its foundations. Had German occupation policy been less brutal and stupid, large portions of the population (especially, but not exclusively, non-Russians) might well have defected from the Soviet state. As it was, hundreds of thousands – if not millions – of soldiers and civilians surrendered or were captured. A large number agreed to serve against the Soviet Union, and many others refused to return there. In the end capitalist allies were needed to help sustain the USSR's military efforts and defeat the enemy.

It is hardly surprising that, even in the exhilaration of victory, Stalin should have had uppermost in his mind not abstract questions about a just and lasting peace settlement, but the fundamental issue of how to prevent such catastrophes from recurring. The territorial buffers he had hurriedly erected in the short period before disaster struck had been of little use. The military preparations he had undertaken had been flawed and inadequate. The 'socialist transformations' implemented in the years between the Revolution and the war had done little, if anything, to inspire in the population loyalty to the regime; the opposite was

closer to the truth, and traditional Russian values and symbols had had to be reintroduced to inspire the populace to sacrifice and heroism.

Throughout the wartime conferences Stalin was determined to assure for the USSR territorial gains that would provide a more effective buffer against attack. Where he did not or could not subsume territory, he operated on the premise that mere hegemony over adjacent land was insufficient and that the political order of such territories itself had to be transformed to fit the Soviet pattern. Either Soviet military occupation or the proximity of Soviet military power facilitated the process – and certainly justified it in Stalin's eyes, whatever the preferences, traditions and other circumstances of the populations involved.

It is not clear whether the establishment of a satellite empire in the form in which it emerged in the late 1940s in Eastern and South-eastern Europe was already clearly part of Stalin's wartime design. The wartime and immediate post-war arguments about Poland indicate that the essentials were clear to Stalin, and he then adapted the pace, intensity and particular methods of the satellization process to the circumstances obtaining in the individual countries concerned. To some degree, he also considered potential foreign reaction. The security concerns of the USSR were thus transformed and expanded to include the security of the new empire and the maintenance of the regimes imposed on the populations with the aid of Moscow-trained Communists. (Czechoslovakia was only marginally exceptional, in the sense that her Communist party, though still a minority, was larger than those of other East European countries. Yugoslavia was a separate case, since the Tito regime had established itself essentially by its own efforts, although Tito and many of his associates also had extensive connections with Moscow.)

Stalin's conception of security in the post-war world, of course, was not confined to the physical protection of the Soviet Union against renewed military threats. Since the safety of the regime, and the political order over which it presided, was of equally crucial concern, especially in the light of wartime events and the dilution of Party orthodoxy, Stalin saw the East European satellite empire as more than a military buffer. He regarded it also as con-

7

stituting the outer lines of defence against various forms of ideological and psychological challenge that emanated from the 'capitalist' world, a wall from behind which conformity could be reimposed only with great difficulty on the peoples of the USSR. This concern with external subversion was almost certainly reinforced by the recognition that the Soviet population would be called upon to make extraordinary sacrifices in terms of their living standards and well-being as the regime pressed forward with reconstructing the industrial base of the country and the maintenance of large military forces. If the East European buffer states were to play this role, it became as essential to identify the survival of their regimes with the physical security of the countries themselves as was the case with the Soviet Union herself. It was, moreover, not sufficient that these regimes should carry the Communist label. (Actually, of course, according to the Soviet ritual, they were not yet Communist regimes but regimes run by Communists, engaged in building socialism as a preliminary to the eventual construction of Communist societies. The Soviet Union herself was said to be still only building socialism.) It was vital that the regimes should be intensely loyal and subservient to the Stalinist regime in Moscow. The designation 'People's Democracy' was attached to each of them and they were instructed to follow the model 'pioneered' by the USSR in the era of socialism in one country. This course carried the seeds of later difficulties.

There had thus emerged an extended concept of security which involved the territorial integrity of both the Soviet Union and the newly acquired empire as well as the ideological and structural conformity of all the parts of the empire and its subordination in all major respects to the needs and concerns of the USSR.

Although the establishment of this empire was portrayed as resulting from a renewal of the revolutionary tide which had subsided after the 1917 Revolution, it had in fact occurred as a result of the use and refinement of largely traditional means of power. Stalin had wielded force, directly and indirectly, to create the empire. But he had not done so indiscriminately; that is, he acted where he judged the risks of doing so to be acceptable in terms of possible Western responses. Later, in 1948–9, when

Yugoslavia failed in several respects to conform to Soviet prescriptions, he was prepared (in his view, perhaps, only temporarily) to overlook one defection because the risks and costs of preventing it seemed to him excessive. This decision probably did not stem so much from fear of Western intervention as from the realization that Tito commanded sufficient support to enable him to put up vigorous resistance to the application of Soviet force.

The question of why Stalin chose to establish buffers in the form of satellites only in Eastern Europe is still open. He had, of course, made demands upon Turkey and Iran, which were designed to provide the USSR with territorial and other advantages associated with security. He had also laid claim to former Italian colonies in the Mediterranean area. But when they were rejected, he refrained from pressing these ambitions, presumably because he considered that resistance might embroil the USSR in complications which he was not then prepared to countenance. In the case of Finland he preferred a form of neutrality and indirect hegemony to satellization, perhaps because he recognized that the establishment of a subservient and conformist pro-Soviet Communist regime would be far more difficult than in Eastern and Southeastern Europe and because he was less certain of Western passivity. He did, of course, impose territorial concessions and other constraints on Finland. In the case of the Far East he held on to territories seized from Japan or Japanese control at the end of the war, but he was not ready to challenge the United States' dominant post-war position on Japan's main islands.

In general, Stalin displayed considerable caution in pressing or undertaking actions which he judged would halt or reverse American withdrawal from the Soviet periphery. The wartime meetings had evidently persuaded him that this was the American intention. Indeed, it was one of the ironies of the split with Yugoslavia that Stalin viewed the latter's intervention in the Greek civil war as potentially detrimental to Soviet security because of possible British and American reactions. Stalin's instinct was right: it was the fragility of the Greek situation, along with fears about the integrity of Turkey, which triggered the first major American decisions leading to the permanent involvement of the United States in Europe.

Stalin displayed similar caution with regard to Communist prospects in France and Italy. He was concerned more with consolidating what he had than with expansion, and he was probably doubtful about whether he could maintain over Communist activities in these more distant areas the kind of control he considered essential in countries adjacent to the USSR. In general, although it was not fully apparent at the time, Stalin had serious doubts about the contribution that would be made to Soviet security by Communist regimes that came to power largely on their own strength. Although Communist theory held that Communist revolutions would be essentially compatible with the Soviet regime, Stalin seems to have been unconvinced. Yugoslavia was already an object lesson; China and Albania were also to defect soon after Stalin died.

Stalin had increased substantially the sphere of dominant Soviet power and had thereby seemingly strengthened the physical security of the USSR. Yet he never lost the siege mentality that had marked Soviet evolution in the 1920s and 1930s. 'Capitalist encirclement' remained for him a reality, both in terms of the military threat to the Soviet Union that he envisaged and in terms of potential connections between internal opposition to the regime and external enemies. Internal repression was therefore as necessary an expedient for him as defence against external aggression.

These very attitudes and the policies they produced resulted in developments which left the position of the USSR considerably less secure than Stalin had hoped. For among the consequences of his policies were the creation of a new Western alliance system, including, after 1950, the permanent stationing of large numbers of American combat forces on the European continent, the gradual incorporation of West Germany in the alliance system and the development of a potent American nuclear arsenal, together with systems capable of delivering these new weapons on to Soviet soil.

From the late 1940s onwards Stalin, facing these developments, had to raise his sights above the consolidation of his homeland and empire to ways of impeding the formation of a potent, new, hostile coalition. This gave rise to the peace movement and its campaigns against the nuclear weaponry that was being acquired by the United States and the alliance system in process of construction in the West. Some of the united-front tactics employed in the 1930s against Hitler were revived, and a certain diplomatic flexibility began to manifest itself – e.g., in the resolution of the Berlin blockade.

Meanwhile, Stalin laid the economic and technological foundation for expanded Soviet military power which looked beyond the defence of the Soviet perimeter and incorporated nuclear weapons in the USSR's military forces. Stalin died as these developments were under way; his successors were left to cope with and build upon them.

Observers of the Stalinist era have pointed out that Stalin's vision was a limited one, coinciding with Soviet artillery range. Within these limits he was, in fact, relatively successful; a dominant position in Eastern Europe, diminished German strength, a weak China and some voice in Japan's future made the USSR relatively more secure than before the war.

Stalin had assumed that the post-war settlement was to be a 'spheres of influence' arrangement. What actually happened, however, was that the USSR's inferior nuclear position inevitably limited her power. At the time, of course, few understood that Stalin was a rather conservative statesman. Western opinion attributed to him and to the USSR the most grandiose aspirations and ambitions. In 1950, in the famous American policy paper, NCS-68, the Soviet Union emerged as a towering giant, casting her shadow over almost all of the world and bent on total conquest. This view was corroborated, shortly after the document was promulgated, by the invasion of Korea. But if Khrushchev is to be believed, this was initially a rather casual affair, with Stalin approving an adventure by Kim Il Sung, which Western statements could have led Stalin to believe was a relatively safe probe. In 12 January 1950 Secretary Acheson had, after all, said the defensive perimeter excluded South Korea.

In short, the immediate post-war period saw the extension of the USSR's security perimeter, but by 1953 the process had about run its course. The limits had been determined first in Iran, then in Greece and Turkey, then in Germany and finally in the Far East.

Few observers would claim that the position of the Soviet Union was 'secure' in 1953. Indeed, Stalin's heirs apparently regarded it as unsatisfactory. In his memoirs Khrushchev gives a summary of this moment: 'We had doubts of our own about Stalin's foreign policy. He over-emphasized the importance of military might for one thing, and consequently put too much faith in our armed forces.' Khrushchev goes on to describe Soviet nervousness over dealing with the Western powers and the Soviet delegation's sense of inferiority in meeting the Western leaders at the Geneva summit in 1955. Yet, freed from Stalin's restraint, his successors began to broaden their horizons and to grope for definitions of security more suited to the emerging situation. For this was no longer simply the post-World War II era, but a time of dramatic changes in military technology and the world political map.

III. THE UNCERTAIN SUPER-POWER: KHRUSHCHEV

It is a commonplace but nevertheless valid contention that the transition from Stalin to Khrushchev reflected the shift from a regional conception of security to a global one, from a basically defensive orientation to an offensive one and from the era of World War II to the nuclear-rocket age.

In the simplest terms, what happened was that Stalin's successors found that it was not only feasible to project Soviet influence beyond the more traditional range of her neighbouring areas, but that this might well pay dividends in terms of the security of the Soviet state. The Soviet Union, however, was quite slow to discover the political consequences of the colonial era's end, having originally regarded newly independent nations like India as likely to remain in the capitalist camp. The process of 'liberation' was already well advanced when Khrushchev and his colleagues began to make their first tentative forays into the Third World.

What did they expect to achieve? The advantages were obvious. If some of the Soviet Union's principal adversaries were caught up in the agonies of relinquishing their colonial holdings, this process might not only be encouraged but could also reinvigorate the broader revolution the older generation had expected, albeit in advanced capitalist countries, thirty years earlier.

Involvement in this process of 'liberation' also had the attraction that in the various struggles the USSR, not the West, was the 'legitimate' power; indeed, it was the USSR that provided a model for transforming relatively weak and backward countries into modern industrial powers, for organizing an economy and forcing its development, and even for reconstructing the social and political order.

Although she was still facing capitalist encirclement in Eurasia, it was thought, the Soviet Union might in turn be able to leap-frog the containment barriers and to encircle the capitalists. A simple calculation revealed that Soviet security – that is, the security of the heartland – would be reinforced if the positions held by the enemy were weakened over a broad front in areas where the Western world still saw its essential reserves.

The story of the USSR's involvement with Nasser, Nehru, Sukarno, etc., need not be rehearsed. But it is worth noting that doctrinal rationalization was elaborated *ex post facto* and piecemeal; the policy was well launched before the 20th Party Congress and the international Communist meetings of the late 1950s.

The very process of elaborating theories concerning 'national democracies' and the like probably reinforced the belief that the policy was, in fact, advantageous. Nevertheless, the fact remains that the Soviet Union's reading of historical development was erroneous. The Soviet model was not widely adopted; local Communists were only marginally effective and sometimes a burden; the West accommodated itself slowly to neutrality; its losses in Asia and Africa were to some extent compensated for by the re-awakening of Western Europe: NATO expanded; Germany began to re-arm; and the treaty of Rome envisaged European unity.

There was also the problem that, as time passed, newly won Soviet advantages and positions had to be reinforced. Stalin had made the complete control of the Eastern European Parties synonymous with Soviet security, permitting no deviations and underwriting his position with the physical presence of the Red Army. This approach was both impracticable and inappropriate to the new era and the regions to which Soviet attention turned. Most of the political forces in these regions were unsuited to the imposition of old-style Comintern discipline and were far from the Soviet homeland. Thus, the Soviet Union was forced to commit herself increasingly to the defence – at least in political and economical terms – of a highly disparate aggregation of states, political parties and movements. And in so doing, she was obliged to accept new obligations and risks in areas where her control was far from complete.

In short, the arena of Soviet security concern expanded and the policy instruments multiplied, but the gains were tenuous and had to be consolidated periodically. In the course of adopting a global policy, the USSR was gradually transforming her techniques in ways that drew on the expertise of her only truly global competitor, the United States.

Indeed, the process of expansion was accompanied inexorably by a growing confrontation with the one power capable of countering the USSR. Where Stalin might have envisaged various political combinations with the capitalists in 1938–9, the range of options available to Khrushchev was more constricted. Soviet security was, above all, defined in terms of competition with the United States. Moreover, that competition was at the highest level a military one. The United States had the longest strategic reach. For the first time the USSR could be threatened directly and devastated by a power that was not bordering on or near her own territory. The nuclear competition could not be affected by 'national liberation' as such; nor was there any firm ideological basis for examining the relationship between the destructiveness of nuclear war and the USSR's political aims.

The problem of adjusting to the nuclear age was obviously a cardinal security issue in the 1950s. It was debated in the military literature and, presumably, in other forums. It had to be confronted during a period of internal tensions and power struggles. What evidence there is suggests that it was one of the issues debated among the various political contenders. Malenkov's deviation, emphasizing the dangers and even the inutility of nuclear war, is well known. It is doubtful that it was an accidental mis-statement. Probably it represented a cautious viewpoint that took account of the possibility, even the necessity, of accommodations with the West. The position that prevailed must have argued for political manoeuvring but involved doctrinal adjustments that avoided the fundamental conflict with Marxist–Leninist prescriptions on war.

The major decisions proclaimed at the 20th Party Congress in 1956 reflected a rather clever compromise. The inevitability of war was qualified: it was no longer 'fatal'; war could be prevented. The means by which it would be circumvented were associated with the new 'social and political forces' that would combine to deter the capitalists. It is worth pausing to note the confusion surrounding the doctrine of the inevitability of war. It stemmed from pre-revolutionary notions concerning relations among capitalist states. The wars that were said to be inevitable were those generated by the inherent antagonisms and conflicts between capitalist states fighting for markets, resources, etc. It was in the era of socialism in one country that the notion was transformed into one applying to relations between socialist and capitalist states. Capitalism, that is, would delay its own demise by resisting forcibly the onward march of socialism. In its original version, the inevitability-of-war doctrine served to benefit the advance of revolution, since the 'peoples' would rebel against the recurrent bloodshed engendered by capitalism and would find their salvation in socialism. As the prospect of intra-capitalist wars seemed to dim after World War II, the emphasis shifted to the inevitability of capitalist–socialist war. Even then, well into the Khrushchev period, the greatest gains of socialism were said to have been the results of the two intra-capitalist world wars (World War II having become a modified socialist–capitalist one only after 1941). The advent of nuclear weapons complicated adherence to the doctrine of inevitable socialist–capitalist war, since it seemed to make the USSR an implicit advocate of such a war. Moreover, if a catastrophic war were inevitable, there was a danger that the Soviet populace would become apathetic and resigned; the 'preventability' of war both allowed for active policies and gave the population hope for prolonged peace.

Meanwhile, Soviet diplomacy would attempt to neutralize the nuclear issue. In effect, what emerged was a more vigorous and diversified version of Stalin's tentative return, in the late 1940s and early 1950s, to some of the popular front approaches of the 1930s. To some extent, Soviet security again became dependent on the manipulation of political forces – Communists, nationalists, neutralists – outside the immediate areas of Soviet control. It was in this context that the principle of 'peaceful coexistence' was revived. It was no doubt viewed as a soporific; it permitted the Soviet leaders to avoid more fundamental choices and it was useful in rationalizing of policies that had already been adopted out of necessity.

But was it wholly tactical? One can only speculate, but it seems plausible that, having resurrected a doctrinal expression to suit their purposes, the Soviet leaders, in continually defining and defending the 'preventability' and coexistence doctrines, found them increasingly comfortable and convenient. Almost certainly, Mao's insistence on the likelihood, and even the desirability, of a cataclysmic showdown found no support in Moscow. In short, tactics blended with strategy. Despite changing external conditions and the growth of Soviet power, the general line of peaceful coexistence has been maintained, and at no point since 1956 has any Soviet leader challenged the contention that a world war was no longer inevitable – nor has there been any real effort to define the limits of the period of coexistence.

To be sure, the Soviet Union recognized that there were fatalistic, passive and defeatist connotations to peaceful coexistence (as well as to the 'inevitability of war'). Enormous energy has been expended on defining what peaceful coexistence is *not* (it does not, for example, exclude 'struggle' or the support of national liberation). Some basic ambiguities have been permitted, and it is this grey area between devastating war and placid peace that has provided Western analysts with endless scope for speculation about real Soviet 'intentions'.

But it is also reasonable to conclude that Khrushchev introduced a period of considerable confusion in Soviet security policy. For one thing, he was entranced by nuclear rockets. The political potential he saw in them emerges clearly from his memoirs, in which he belittles 'rifles and bayonets' and claims that the USSR's defence depends on the 'quality and quantity of our nuclear missile arsenal'. The Soviet warning to Britain and France in the Suez crisis of 1956 foreshadowed the more aggressive conduct of the USSR after 1957. Not only could the Soviet Union compensate for intercontinental inferiority by holding Europe hostage, but the threat of a 'missile gap' offered a chance to achieve some of the recurrent Soviet aims in a period of offensive pressures. Thus Khrushchev's demands in 1958–60 were strikingly reminiscent of earlier Soviet demands: the exclusion of the West from Berlin and final settlement of the German problem.

The events of the period cannot be recounted here. Khrushchev ran a gigantic bluff that became increasingly complicated and dangerous. In some desperation, he sought a breakthrough by means of a bold stroke in Cuba. He failed and thereby brought the optimistic and most assertive phase of his policy to a close.

Any assessment of Soviet security in the Khrushchev period must note some major internal developments and the state of international Communism. First, the initial 'thaw', the subsequent de-Stalinization and the disappearance of mass terror had a bearing on security problems. Stalin's successors were less paranoid, though still concerned about internal enemies. Having lived through the various plots and counter-plots concocted by Stalin, they must have concluded that the internal threat was exaggerated. In the light of what happened in Poland and Hungary, however, one must ask why Khrushchev launched his internal repudiation of Stalin. Moreover, why did he promote the reconciliation with Tito, going so far as to revise the doctrine of a single road to socialism?

It is important to remember that de-Stalinization and internal liberalization were by no means unanimously supported policies; they were resisted at very high levels and were thus instruments in Politburo struggles. Most important, de-Stalinization was not a process which the Soviet Union had foreseen in all its consequences once it had spread outside her borders. Far from operating on a master plan, it seems probable that the Soviet Union became engaged in a series of *ad hoc* decisions and struggles. De-Stalinization was a weapon against Malenkov and Molotov. The reconciliations with Tito accorded with the same strategy.

In retrospect, the various cross-currents of domestic and foreign policy were much stronger throughout Khrushchev's period than was generally recognized. Much as Stalin feared that his 'enemies' had never accepted the legitimacy of his own rule, Khrushchev continued to see 'Stalinists', or at least professed to see them, as his principal opponents. Thus his policies, which might otherwise have seemed reasonable, were often justified and defended in strident and dogmatic terms. His obsession with Stalin, which comes through in his memoirs, had the effect of driving him to extremes; his own apprehensions compounded his tendency to over-react and over-achieve.

Indeed, it may be that Khrushchev felt driven to prove that his anti-Stalinism would be crowned with success: where Stalin ignored the Third World, Khrushchev courted it; where Stalin insisted on iron rule, Khrushchev proclaimed relaxations; where Stalin ruled Eastern Europe through the army and the KGB, Khrushchev hoped for loyalty to principles; where Stalin sought security in the Red Army, Khrushchev sought it in the strategic rocket forces (though he bluffed about their strength). The result was that Khrushchev defined Soviet interests so broadly that he became over-committed and some breakdown or retrenchment was probably inevitable.

One can only speculate about the extent to which Khrushchev was also driven by his resentment or fear of China. Khrushchev claims in his memoirs that he told his comrades as early as 1954 that conflict with China was 'inevitable'. Whether or not this is true, his policies hastened the conflict. It is likely that by 1959, when China claims Khrushchev halted Soviet assistance for her nuclear weapons programme, China had acquired the status of an adversary, if not an outright enemy. This was not fully appreciated at the time; until 1964 it was believed in the West that there was a continuing prospect of a Soviet-Chinese reconciliation. Since the split was fully confirmed after Khrushchev's fall, it is probable that his antipathy towards or apprehensions about China were not personal predilections but reflected a new dimension of Soviet security concerns.

A review of the Khrushchev period proffers certain conclusions. First, the Soviet Union began to view her security in much broader geographical and functional terms, and in doing so she accepted commitments and risks that made the management of national security policy more complex. Second, the nuclear issue assumed more urgency and the competition with the United States came to be judged more and more in terms of the strategic nuclear balance. Third, the relaxation of tension inside the USSR accelerated centrifugal tendencies in the Communist orbit, leading to a partial reconciliation with, but also concessions to, Yugoslavia and a deepening split with China – in effect stimulating pluralism. Fourth, the shift from regionalism to globalism cost the Soviet Union a good deal: it imposed new military-economic burdens but yielded only a marginal weakening of the regime's main adversaries abroad. By 1964 national security for the USSR was a complex equation. It involved calculations concerning the internal repercussion of foreign policies, the cost of sustaining large economic and political commitments in Eastern Europe as well as in much more remote areas, the burden of armaments to offset Western build-ups and the ideological and doctrinal consequences of the era of disintegrating Communist ranks. In this light, it is not surprising that more elements of the Soviet bureaucracy, particularly the military, were drawn into policy deliberations.

IV. THE ACCUMULATION OF POWER: BREZHNEV

We do not have access to any systematic, internal Soviet definition of the security status of the USSR in the mid-1960s. Nor can we say precisely how the Soviet Union defined the notion of security at that point in her history.

If security is to be regarded chiefly as a function of military power, the Soviet sense of security must have been substantially greater then than at any other time in the country's history. Security (defined as safety from imminent attack) was certainly greater than in the past. It should be observed, however, that even in the mid- and late 1920s, as well as in the 1940s, when the USSR's military power was much less formidable, her security concerns revolved chiefly around a generally hostile environment which might, over a longer or shorter period of time, evolve towards active aggression – or, more accurately, towards active resistance to Soviet incursion. Soviet fears of imminent, active aggression were justifiably greatest in the late 1930s, as intensive German rearmament proceeded amidst violent hostility against Bolshevism, thinly disguised claims to 'living space' adjacent to or even within the USSR, and in the context of the anti-Comintern pact. In the post-war world there may have been intermittent fears of imminent strategic attack, but they were associated with crises often caused by the USSR's own actions.

By any measure Soviet power had vastly increased between 1945 and 1965. Ground and air forces had been modernized and were deployed in substantial numbers in all areas where attacks might conceivably occur (with some exceptions in the Far East). Large reserves were maintained. The navy was in the process of evolving from a coastal defence force designed to support a land battle to one that could be used, at least for purposes of showing the flag, in more remote places. A squadron was permanently deployed in the Mediterranean and some facilities were available in Cuba. Plans were under way to increase and diversify the navy and to enlarge the merchant marine. Long-range intervention forces, in the form of air transports, airborne divisions and amphibious forces, were making their appearance. Strategic forces, though numerically and technically inferior to those of the United States, were growing with sustained momentum and were losing their initial vulnerability to preemptive or preventive strikes by the United States. Industry and technology were harnessed to a permanent effort to maintain and improve these forces.

These developments in their totality had begun to place a serious question mark over Western strategy for the defence of Europe. The West could no longer place unqualified reliance on the first use of nuclear weapons to compensate for disadvantages in conventional theatre forces and for extended over-water lines of communication. In addition, at this stage the United States was increasingly preoccupied with the war in Vietnam, which deflected forces

and energies from the power competition with the USSR. The Soviet Union almost certainly considered it in her interest to see the United States thus diverted, although that judgment came gradually to be qualified. Along with this preoccupation in Asia, the United States found her presence and influence in the Middle East seriously impaired after the 1967 war, largely – but not wholly – to the benefit of the USSR.

But if these trends in the power equation were a necessary condition, they still did not turn out to be a sufficient condition for security. For one thing, despite her enormous gains in power, the Soviet Union remained obsessed by the notion of inequality. She still saw the United States as an established world power and herself merely as an aspiring one. American influence, although less imposing than before and despite declining relative military power, remained widespread and deepseated. Soviet influence, meanwhile, was increasing generally but continued to fluctuate and it seemed much less secure than that of the United States and, indeed, of other physically much weaker Western powers. Economic and cultural ties between the West and the Third World, although often challenged by the latter, still seemed more durable than similar ties between the USSR and the Third World. The appeals of Soviet ideology were more superficial than real; political ties were vulnerable to changes in third-world regimes and nationalist resistance. Soviet efforts at transforming positions of influence into outposts of power (and hence security) frequently met only temporary success and at times outright failure.

Closer to home, Soviet power and a quarter of a century of Communist rule had failed to eradicate strivings for national identity in Eastern Europe. Beneath the crust of Stalinism – and probably encouraged by it – popular hostility towards the Soviet Union and resistance to imposed uniformity grew. The regional economic, military and political structures which Khrushchev had sought to substitute for crude and direct domination had not produced the commonwealth of which he had dreamt. If anything, centrifugal forces revived with renewed force. If, as the Soviet Union argued, her power was forcing the West to accept a form of peaceful coexistence, this very evolution also increased the pressures in

Eastern Europe to renew earlier ties with the Western world and to reduce dependence on the USSR. The Prague Spring in 1968 demonstrated that popular resistance to incorporation in the Soviet order remained a strong, latent force, ready to erupt in defiance of virtually certain Soviet military action calculated to crush it.

These trends, and the diverse expression they found in the several East European countries, showed that continued Soviet dominance did not necessarily spell control of events. Interestingly enough, it was in the face of these realities that Khrushchev's successors set out in the late 1960s to seek Western confirmation of Soviet hegemony in Eastern Europe. (The renewed pressures for a European security conference and for confirmation of the 'results of World War II' clearly had this intent.) Ironically, the Soviet Union thus sought legitimacy for her position from her putative enemies. The Soviet Union no doubt believed that her power entitled her to this. Ironically, her allies in the West, the Communist parties, found it difficult to offer help unreservedly to the Soviet Union. By this time, these parties were seeking increasing voter acceptance by demonstrating, in form if not in substance, that the era of total subservience to the USSR had ended in the international Communist movement.

In many ways, the persistent and mounting challenge from Peking was an even more serious threat to the sense of security which great and growing power might have conferred upon the Soviet Union. Here was not only a separate and competing pole of attraction and orthodoxy in the Communist world; Peking also challenged the Soviet quest for influence and recognition in the Third World. More than that: although she was backward in terms of modern military capacity, China voiced claims to Soviet territory and did not shrink from frontier altercations. If the Soviet Union approached the rest of the world with a sense of grievance over real and imagined wrongs perpetrated on her and her Tsarist predecessors, China managed to place the Soviet Union on the defensive by identifying her with 'unequal' treaties of the past. Whatever the turmoil of the 'Great Leap Forward' and the 'Cultural Revolution', the Soviet Union could not shake off the nightmare of

nearly a thousand million determined people eventually gaining the power to seek to redress the wrongs of the distant and recent past. The dream of non-antagonistic contradictions had long since evaporated, and there was scant comfort in the claim that the Chinese leaders had left the path of Marxism–Leninism. The USSR could retain intact the illusion that there can be no basic conflict between genuine revolutionaries, but she could not ignore the fact that here was a hostile power abutting on millions of square kilometres of rich but sparsely populated Soviet land, which was linked with European Russia by fragile communications and peopled at the rim by non-Russians whose affinity with Muscovite rule had its own historic uncertainties.

The accumulation of military force and the extension of its reach beyond the Eurasian landmass thus had not overcome some of the inherent flaws in the polity that the Soviet rulers had constructed over half a century. At the same time, the sense of power conferred on the Soviet Union by the steady shift in the military balance increased the Soviet appetite for tangible and intangible pay-offs. As in the past, this appetite had its defensive as well as offensive elements. But, for the first time since the Revolution, aspiration was being buttressed by great and growing power. In this respect, the late 1960s (and the period since then) differed from the optimistic phase of Khrushchev's term of office. While he was fascinated by modern weaponry, he had, like others before him, seen as the most potent sources of growing Soviet influence the nature of the Soviet system and the supposed confluence of revolutionary currents. His successors seemed less sanguine on these counts and relied more on the (by then) cumulative impact of raw power. It was not so much that they intended to use this power directly, although they plainly did not exclude that possibility; they believed, rather, that power would pay political dividends. Indeed, they believed that the USSR was entitled to these dividends; that she was entitled to be treated and respected as a super-power; and that this role should be given formal recognition through treaties and understandings, above all with the United States.

The Soviet concept of security thus became closely associated with the concept of equality and with the determination that the USSR should have her rights of access, presence and influence acknowledged on a world-wide basis in form as well as substance. As power grew, so did the definition of security. The safety of the homeland was the principal consideration; the inviolability of Soviet predominance in Eastern Europe was a close second; 'friendly' powers elsewhere on the Soviet periphery were next; and entitlement to a role at least equal to that of the United States elsewhere came last.

Yet the implementation of such plans was problematic. The homeland was safe from land attack, but it could not be protected either from vast destruction if nuclear war should break out or from infection by alien ideas. Eastern Europe was in the Soviet camp but full of cross-currents which diluted Soviet control. While Soviet power based in the area aimed an arrow at the West, the region was also an avenue for Western influence. Other countries on the periphery, while not actively hostile towards the Soviet Union, were far from friendly and were not deterred from maintaining and building military forces and alliances that enabled them to resist Soviet pressures. China was hostile, an active rival and, in Soviet eyes, potentially a long-term physical threat. Japan was moderately friendly but hardly supine. Further afield the Soviet presence was growing but remained contested and uneven.

Security had thus become a goal whose attainment would require ever-increasing measures of military power and unceasing effort. As Soviet security was being defined in terms of the security situation of the United States – the Soviet Union was now demanding 'equal security' – commitment to it was increasingly open-ended. Even if Soviet missile forces reached rough numerical parity with those of the United States, as they did in the late 1960s, that still did not spell a condition of equality. For American missile technology was more advanced than that of the Soviet Union; the USSR faced not only the United States but Britain and France as well, who represented the 'forward-based' systems of the United States; and the USSR needed strategic forces to act as a threat (or deterrent) to China. If Soviet ground forces were substantially more extensive than those of the United States, the USSR was still not in a position of parity *vis-à-vis* the United States,

because the latter had no land enemy comparable with China. Indeed, wherever the Soviet Union looked she seemed to feel herself in need of 'compensation', either for discriminations and disadvantages suffered in the past, or for contemporary or future ones. A natural consequence of this outlook was that as 'compensation' was piled on 'compensation', the United States and others against whom the Soviet Union measured her security considered their own interests to be in jeopardy and undertook a variety of counter-actions which in turn established new military requirements for the USSR. (It should be noted that during the Vietnam war particularly, but at other times too, the United States and her allies did not, in fact, respond to all accretions in Soviet power. Indeed, real defence outlays, apart from Vietnam-related expenses, declined steadily during the 1960s and 1970s. Moreover, with increasing personnel costs, outlays on military hardware declined even more sharply. Individual programmes, such as the introduction of multiple independently-targetable re-entry vehicles (MIRV) in American land- and sea- based missile forces, did proceed, however.)

Brezhnev and his colleagues had thus inherited from Khrushchev the conviction that the Soviet Union could not and should not be satisfied with securing the borders of the homeland and its Western outposts, but should strive for a status resembling that of the United States. Khrushchev had had the notion that the Soviet Union could match and overtake the economic strength of the United States and that this would render the Soviet example irresistible elsewhere in the world. Military power, which Khrushchev did not neglect but which he had tried to channel into particular areas, would be the concomitant of economic power and the power of example. Brezhnev was realistic enough to see the failings of this conception. Once he had consolidated his political position at home, he muted the themes of economic and ideological competition and generally sought to avoid head-on collisions with the USSR's principal antagonists, the United States and China. He proceeded methodically to build Soviet military power in all its dimensions and, having failed in his overtures to China and then in efforts to contain and surround her with Soviet allies, shifted to an 'opening to the West'. It was this strategy that was shaped in the period leading up to the 24th Communist Party Congress in 1971 and proclaimed in programmatic terms on that occasion.

Defence and Security

The unveiling of the 'peace programme' of the 24th Party Congress marked the start of the present period. It has been characterized by a continuation of older political-security concerns, especially in Europe, by some new elements, especially in relations with the United States, and by some enduring uncertainties over China and Asia and over the question of leadership succession. Above all, it has been a period in which commitment to the growth of the Soviet Union's military power has become an increasingly predominant characteristic of the regime. This has raised persistent questions abroad about Soviet intentions – about how the USSR will conduct her policies in an era of military parity, if not superiority.

By the time of the 24th Party Congress, the 'detente' with the Federal Republic of Germany was well advanced. The Eastern treaties were a culmination of post-war aims to ratify the *status quo*, although they were by no means entirely the product of skilful Soviet policy; changes in West Germany played a considerable role in the conclusion of the treaties and the Soviet Union prudently worked with the new forces. But the consolidation of a European detente, as defined by the USSR, proved elusive. The West introduced new demands involving respect for human rights and increased contacts at the very time when the older issues of territorial integrity, recognition of borders, etc., were being settled. And at the same time, the willingness of the Soviet Union to temper or resist these new trends was inhibited by her growing economic interest in securing trade and credits from West Europe. A reversion to harsher Soviet alternatives in Europe would thus entail economic losses that might not seem justified by any political advantages to be gained from taking a harder line. On the other hand, the Soviet Union faced the dilemma of whether or not she should risk the further military relaxation in Europe which the West was demanding ever more insistently.

Soviet superiority in conventional military forces, of course, has been an essential support for Soviet policy since 1945. But this advantage clearly raises for the Western partners the question of the terms for continuing the European detente, especially as each cycle of force modernization seems to create new advances. A persistent Western search for some means to eliminate some, if not all, of the USSR's conventional military advantages could pose problems which Soviet regimes in the past have managed to evade. The basic security issue is whether the Soviet Union could afford to compete and coexist in Europe under conditions of near parity of conventional forces in Central Europe. Could she, in fact, withdraw large numbers of her forces as a result of a negotiated settlement, or agree to stabilize a regional balance of nuclear forces? How would this affect her security interests in Eastern Europe?

How these questions are eventually answered will depend in part on the Soviet perception of the China problem. A prominent analytical line is that the Soviet Union has sought a period of relaxation in the West in order to consolidate her build-up in the East. This is plausible and consistent with the evidence provided by the share of Soviet military resources devoted to China. But it is an explanation more of tactics than of a well-defined strategy. What does the Soviet Union do in the post-Mao period?

It seems likely that at one time the USSR harboured hopes that after Mao a *modus vivendi* could be agreed with China; while this is still possible, especially given the propensity for internal turmoil in the Chinese leadership, the entire relationship seems to be shifting to a new level of geo-political competition ushered in by the Chinese economic modernization programme, the Sino-Japanese treaty, the conflict in Indochina and normalization with the US.

We can only note that the Soviet treaty with North Vietnam is a new element in Soviet security policy; it has antecedents in friendship treaties with several third-world countries, but the Soviet Union could not have been oblivious to the risk that this particular treaty might become a blank cheque. At present all that can be hazarded is that the odds on a confrontation with China are now shorter. The prospect of Western willingness to underwrite Chinese economic and military modernization must raise the old spectre of encirclement. It also raises the question of whether and which Soviet policies will be adopted to break up a hostile coalition. 'Encirclement' clearly does not accord with the regime's appreciation of Soviet power and its consequent demand for 'equal security'. Soviet leaders must be asking themselves whether they can accept a policy of detente with the West which could lead to an underwriting of Chinese armament efforts by the USSR's European detente partners.

The question of how to manage a European detente and a Chinese confrontation inevitably involves a consideration of Soviet policy towards the United States. The decision taken in the early 1970s to enter into a period of relaxation with Washington was not a sudden one. The factors which appear to have prompted the decision are: (1) the conclusion of the Eastern treaties, which required a further payment in the Berlin negotiations that involved the United States; (2) the American opening to China in 1971, which helped to produce the American–Soviet summit of 1972; (3) the prospect of an anti-ballistic missile (ABM) race; (4) economic needs; and (5) the ascendency of Brezhnev. All (except perhaps the last factor) necessitated an active policy of manoeuvre.

Of course, the Soviet Union expected dividends, primarily in the form of economic assistance, which she needed in a period of intensive economic development requiring major inputs of capital and technology, but also in the form of the curtailment of certain areas of strategic competition. Having embarked on the detente policy, the Soviet Union found that, as it evolved, she could not disengage herself from it, even though it yielded smaller dividends than expected and elicited new challenges.

The point is that the Soviet Union became to some extent the prisoner of her own commitments. Having proclaimed the irreversibility of detente, she could not easily dismiss it as a temporary aberration without calling into question the judgment of her own leadership. Having entered into the Strategic Arms Limitation Talks (SALT) negotiations and signed one treaty of indefinite duration, she could not easily jettison the process, even though it had become more complex. Having committed herself to multi-billion dollar programmes, she could not run political risks that could jeopardize them.

This is not to say that the Soviet Union has been straining to abandon the line of the 24th Party Congress. Brezhnev's personal identification with it is a powerful impediment to such a course. Moreover, new gains have been achieved, and others may be looming. In Africa, in particular, the Soviet Union has found a novel approach to the projection of her power – through proxy military forces. This was foreshadowed to some extent in the Middle East, when Soviet forces were in combat along the Suez line during the tensions of 1970–1. But the stationing abroad of sizeable forces of a Soviet ally is new; it provides new leverage in an area of major Western concerns. The impressive fact is that the Soviet Union has accepted the concomitant risks with apparent equanimity. The two incursions – in Angola and in Ethiopia – thus suggest that the Soviet Union has already reappraised the opportunities and inhibitions of a more forward policy. The most intriguing question is whether this reappraisal reflects only an assessment of local conditions or a broader evaluation of a change in the overall balance of power.

In any case, the more traditional notion of security relating to the periphery of the USSR has probably received a new impetus by events along her southern periphery, particularly in Afghanistan, but also in Turkey and Iran. At present, the situation in Iran is uncertain. The Soviet Union has played a cautious hand – in part because of her interest in a continuous flow of natural gas, in part because the religiously motivated opponents of the Shah could have undesired effects on the USSR's own Muslim population, and in part because the Soviet Union has probably not yet seen an effective indigenous Iranian force with which to ally herself. Nevertheless, she has issued solemn warnings against foreign intervention, asserting her own state security interests because of the proximity of her borders. Moscow is probably as uncertain about the future course of events as anyone, but it must at least be harbouring hopes of, and possibly taking some action to encourage, a more congenial regime in an area which Russians have historically viewed with a mixture of fear and ambition.

At the same time, the peace programme of the 24th Party Congress has suffered the effects of a number of events, some well beyond Soviet control: the resignations of Brandt and Nixon; Soviet expulsion from the Middle East and the revival of American presence and influence there; the modest economic benefits of relations with the United States; and the reappearance of human rights as an international political issue.

The Soviet Union has thus encountered some serious contradictions. On the one hand, her military power has grown both absolutely and relatively. Her reach has made itself felt in distant places, and favourable tides may be running on the USSR's southern rim. On the other hand, there is a budding relationship among the Soviet Union's principal adversaries – Western Europe, Japan, China and the United States. The Soviet Union seems to recognize this, but how she will handle it is far from clear. At present she appears to be still at the stage of issuing 'serious' warnings.

Yet it must be clear to the Soviet regime that the USSR has been able neither to translate her military preponderance into lasting favourable political alignments nor to neutralize alignments she considers inimical. Thus the curious paradox of strategic nuclear power seems to have affected the Soviet Union perhaps even more than it has affected the United States.

Finally, it is obvious that for more than a decade Soviet security has been defined and presided over by a group of leaders who will not survive more than a few more years. One can only speculate about the turmoil that the change of leaders will provoke. The most fascinating aspect is that a new leadership will inherit a position of far greater power than any of its predecessors; but it will also inherit a new set of problems, particularly in the management of economic resources, which in part is the price to be paid for the massive increases in Soviet power.

V. THE PROBLEM OF MILITARY POWER

One of the themes of the foregoing sections is that the Soviet Union has oscillated between periods of expansion and periods of consolidation, and that in the process the more or less constant concern about the security of her periphery has coexisted with a new, more extensive complex of interests which are harder to define. It is difficult to establish a close correlation between periods of retrenchment or expansion and the balance of military power. There have only been two brief periods – 1946–7 and during the 1957–9 'missile gap' – when the Soviet Union has enjoyed temporary military advantages. In the first period, she made major gains; the second proved to be less politically exploitable. But for most of her 61 years, while political gains varied, she has operated from a position of relative military weakness.

Almost all observers have concluded that this position has now changed, and the debate has shifted to the question of Soviet goals – parity or 'superiority'? This debate has raised the more dramatic question of whether the Soviet Union has come to view war quite differently from the West; more precisely, does she consider herself as deterred from initiating, or even risking, a nuclear war, or does she see such a war as not only conceivable but 'winnable'?

A number of factors are involved. First, myriads of technical decisions are made by every major military power, and no political leadership is capable of monitoring all of them. In this sense such decisions clearly have some bureaucratic momentum distinct from the needs of grand strategy. Second, the long lead times involved in creating modern weapons creates a gap between technical decisions and their strategic rationale. Current Soviet strategic forces are clearly evolutionary; in some measure they were planned and developed under Khrushchev. Two major Soviet intercontinental ballistic missiles (ICBM), the SS-9 and SS-11, were clearly products of the Khrushchev era and represent the refinement of the technologies of the late 1950s. The Brezhnev politburo authorized further refinements and improvements and probably set the overall force levels, partly through unilateral decisions but also as a result of bargaining in SALT. Thus it can be misleading to conclude from technical aspects, numbers or characteristics that these weapons necessarily reflect a concerted, long-term strategy.

Even if they do represent some coherent approach evolved over time, as seems likely, the problem of perspective is important. How does the Soviet Union draw strategic conclusions from a comparison of forces? We tend to impute to Soviet analysts what seems a reasonable Western framework. Western pre-occupation with SALT has further skewed the issue; most strategic comparisons accept the SALT framework of certain missiles and heavy bombers, but there is some evidence that the Soviet Union views the balance in larger, more geo-political terms. Her complaints about allied nuclear weapons systems and American forward bases have a tactical rationale in SALT polemics, but it would be surprising if these aspects are dismissed in Soviet military analysis. There is little incentive for Soviet marshals to make out the best case for themselves, and, in a country in which resources are always scarce, there is every incentive to put in a claim based on the worst case. Moreover, in the Soviet Union, unlike in the West, there is no counter-analysis, for no bureaucratic element has access to the kind of information that is involved in force comparisons. In short, the system is tilted towards a large military effort with considerable momentum, and only a strong, dominant leader could check or reverse these inherent tendencies.

The problem of 'doctrine', however, remains. The analysis is coloured in some degree by Western use of 'evidence'. Official writings are given great weight. It is argued from this evidence that the Soviet Union does not accept the concept of mutual assured destruction. She probably does not, if only because it implies a political equivalence between herself and her enemies. It is a purely Western concept, reflecting Western values and attitudes. It is unlikely that the Soviet Union would simply adopt it without qualifying it with political considerations. Thus, the Soviet leaders freely and frequently acknowledge the destructiveness of nuclear war, but they carefully stop short of concluding that this fact alone makes a nuclear conflict unthinkable. To do so would be to refute certain fundamental views of the nature of capitalism on which the Soviet Union insists.

But it is legitimate to ask what the Soviet Union does believe. It is currently fashionable to assert that she believes that nuclear war is not only conceivable but also 'winnable', and that Soviet policy is dedicated to producing forces that create optimal conditions for 'victory' in a nuclear conflict. Recently, this view has been advanced with vigour in various articles, even though the body of evidence is not new. In these descriptions Soviet policy is made to appear radically different from that of the West. On the surface this may seem persuasive, but certain questions are nevertheless posed. Is 'warfighting', for example, a purely Soviet concept, unknown in the West? The fact is that almost every American (and Western) strategic system has some combat rationale. At bottom the chief difference seems to lie in the strategy of striking first, either deliberately or pre-emptively, or simply retaliating. Since Khrushchev, the Soviet Union has asserted that the first phase of a nuclear exchange will be decisive in determining the strategic goals of the opposing sides. It follows that striking first may confer significant advantages, which the experience of the Soviet Union in 1941 demonstrated. Thus, competition for advantages in an initial exchange seems to be basic to Soviet doctrine.

Even so, one cannot fail to note that evidence for many points of Soviet doctrine is either non-existent or carefully concealed. There is virtually no explicit evidence of what Soviet war aims would be, what would constitute victory, how wars would terminate, or what the coalitions and alignments would be. Would the USSR strike both the United States and China simultaneously? Does she assume war will be global, even if she attacks only in the West? If so, what does this mean in terms of the analysis of her force requirements? In short, a complete perspective is lacking.

It is probable that Soviet analysis of nuclear war in all its aspects is more dynamic than Western analysis claims. The Soviet Union has been engaged in debate, and there are unlikely to be definitive answers. The debates continue among Soviet military figures, between political and military leaders and perhaps among the political leaders themselves. One reason for this fluid state of affairs is that the personnel involved probably have their biases. Political figures of Brezhnev's generation cannot simply discard the psychological baggage of decades and alter their mode of thought. Their experience tells them that military balances may be transitory. They appreciate raw military power, and have demonstrated that they are willing to use it to protect vital interests, and to threaten to use it to protect their wider 'security interests'. But this is still several steps short of believing that an overall balance of strategic and regional advantage exists that is politically exploitable as far as threatening nuclear war.

The more important questions are whether they or their successors may come to believe in the 1980s that the overall balance has shifted decisively and, if they believe that it has, whether they will demand commensurate geo-political adjustments and, should that expedient fail, whether they will resort to the open use of force.

These questions, which are becoming more urgent in the West, raise parallel questions about the value of arms-control negotiations in forestalling certain Soviet threats as well as in alleviating legitimate Soviet anxieties.

VI. THE ROLE OF ARMS CONTROL IN SOVIET SECURITY

Since the first days of the Revolution, disarmament proposals and agitation have played a prominent role in Soviet policy. The Bolsheviks sensed the thirst for peace among virtually all of the participants in World War I and they quickly identified themselves with it. It served them both as an incentive with which to revolutionize the masses and as the great goal of the Revolution.

It was only natural that before long the promotion of peace should be accompanied and reinforced by advocacy of the abolition of armaments. As Marxists, Bolsheviks knew that capitalists thrived on the manufacture of arms (though in the end this would only hasten the demise of the capitalist system), and that to abolish the arms business would strike a mortal blow at the class enemy and would deprive the latter of its only means of resisting the revolutionary flood tide.

But the assumptions and hopes of the revolutionary period soon had to give way to the imperatives of a Soviet state surrounded by hostile forces. Where peace and disarmament had been the slogans of revolution, they now became weapons in the battle to hold the external world at bay.

It often came to be said of Soviet disarmament proposals and campaigns in later years that they were 'mere' propaganda. With their utopian content and agitational form, no doubt they were, but they were also more than that, because they served the very concrete purposes, during times of weakness and danger, of disorienting potential enemies, giving Communists a rallying cause and showing the Soviet people that their leaders stood for great ideals, even though they were obliged to impose cruel sacrifices on the workers and peasants.

From the beginning Soviet disarmament policy was, in fact, an instrument of strategy, even when it was propounded as an end in itself. In this respect the Soviet Union has always been ahead of the West. Her national security policy has incorporated disarmament policy rather than being seen as in conflict with it. Despite the massive efforts devoted to the subject by Soviet media, diplomats and leaders, there has never been a disarmament (or arms-control) 'community' or, for that matter, a separate government agency concerned with it.

It must, of course, be stressed that the Soviet Union was chiefly concerned, at least until the mid-1950s, with the advocacy of disarmament rather than with the actual military implications of their proposals. She readily engaged in frequent and intensive negotiations after the establishment of the United Nations but she was more concerned with the process than with the outcome. Negotiating on nuclear issues from a position of weakness in the 1940s, the Soviet Union was very clear that the negotiating process should be used to gain time and to generate the political climate in which she could acquire the weapon which Stalin had once nonchalantly described as useful only for playing on people's weak nerves. It is doubtful in the extreme that Stalin ever thought there was the slightest possibility that the United States would accept or even seriously talk about the elaborate but unenforceable Soviet proposals for the prohibition of nuclear weapons. And he must occasionally have wondered what made anyone in the West think that the Soviet Union would ever have entertained the Baruch Plan, which called for the international control of atomic energy with a view to eliminating all atomic weapons. The Soviet response had been to demand a ban on production, storage and use of nuclear weapons and for their destruction *before* the introduction of control measures.[1] While working to build up his own arsenal, Stalin used the deadlocked negotiations to stigmatize nuclear weaponry so that forceful restraints would inhibit any American leader who might contemplate its use against the USSR. The peace campaigns of the late 1940s that led up to the climactic Stockholm Appeal in 1950 were almost certainly mounted in close co-ordination with the management of the crises over the Berlin Blockade and the start of the Korean war. Throughout that war, the Soviet and Soviet-controlled agitation machinery worked intensively to propagate the Stockholm Appeal. It would be interesting to see from Soviet archives (were they ever to be available) to what extent American hints dropped in 1953 that nuclear weapons might nevertheless be used contributed to the eventual termination of the Korean war after Stalin's death.

Sometime during the early Khrushchev era, the Soviet Union apparently began to pay more serious attention to the content of disarmament negotiations and to the situation that would arise were one or another of these negotiations to reach a conclusion. It is worth recalling that in 1955, despite her long history of utopian proposals and her periodic reversion to them, it was the Soviet Union who came to grips for the first time with the fact that by then it had probably become technically impossible to enforce a total ban on nuclear weapons. The Soviet proposals of May 1955 were a landmark not because they indicated some sort of breakthrough to success in negotiations, but because they recognized that nuclear weapons were here to stay. And that, no doubt, reflected Khrushchev's conclusion that these weapons would become a mainstay of Soviet military power. (It may be observed that a similar note of realism had been sounded in 1954 by the initial Soviet response to President Eisenhower's Atoms for Peace proposal. Molotov pointed out that any such scheme raised the danger of the diversion of such technology to military purposes. The Soviet Union had little difficulty in detecting the dangers to her security from such diversions, and she has never wavered in her belief in non-proliferation, even if her practices have not always been completely consistent with it.)

While committing the Soviet Union irreversibly to nuclear weaponry, Khrushchev and his associates took the first tentative steps towards considering the possibility that in the nuclear age antagonists might take certain actions to reassure each other. The 1955 proposals on surprise attack, while technically deficient and one-sided, constituted nevertheless the first concrete Soviet initiative suggesting some sort of foreign control on Soviet soil.

We cannot review here the history of arms-control negotiations since the 1950s, but we believe it can be demonstrated that, just as the Soviet Union had pursued concrete security goals, in the essentially agitational phase of her disarmament policy, so these aims predominated as agitation came gradually to be accompanied by actual negotiation. The point should not be misunderstood: it is not that the Soviet Union saw in arms control an alternative to military power, but that she regarded the former as an adjunct of the latter, and both as serving the security needs of the country.

More specifically, the Soviet Union probably adopted a more serious negotiating posture in the late 1950s and early 1960s because she had come to recognize that agitation alone would not seriously impede US military programmes or Western military strategies that envisaged the use of nuclear weapons in the event of regional war, especially in Europe. It may even be possible that she believed that continual and extensive use of agitational techniques might hamper her own programmes, or at least generate unnecessary political costs. A more credible negotiating posture would alleviate any problems of the latter kind but, more important, it could well have a more telling effect in the West.

In short, the Soviet Union saw in the negotiating route a possible way of curtailing Western programmes and dispositions that tended to offset the gains the USSR had herself been making in bringing about a more satisfactory military balance, especially as regards nuclear and strategic weapons. In taking this route she recognized that limitations would have to be mutual and this confronted her with complex cost-benefit judgments about particular negotiating outcomes. Almost certainly, differences of view arose among Soviet leaders, military and civilian, and between some military officers and civilian leaders. Evidence of this is presumptive rather than conclusive, but it is not unreasonable to suppose, in connection with the first SALT agreement in 1972, that Brezhnev and his Politburo allies may have over-ruled others who were reluctant to give up insistence on curtailment of American forward-based systems (FBS). For Brezhnev, the principal achievement of 1972 was almost certainly the suspension of the American ABM programme, and he was not inclined to jeopardize this by sticking on the FBS issue. He faced a somewhat similar situation at the Vladivostok summit with President Ford (see *Survival*, Sept./Oct. 1974, pp. 232–8) in 1974, when he decided once again to do without curtailments of FBS in order to obtain what then looked like a ten-year projection of the strategic balance which would facilitate Soviet economic and military planning. Soviet readiness to reach agreement without reducing the FBS threat – strictly speaking, the 'traditional' FBS threat, since the Soviet Union did seek to curb cruise missiles which already might conceivably have been viewed in 1974 as a new form of FBS – may well have been justified on the grounds that the USSR's own non-central nuclear delivery systems were increasingly offsetting and over-matching the relatively limited number of Western 'theatre' systems capable of effective attack against Soviet territory.

We cannot tell precisely to what extent the limits on Soviet forces required under SALT I curtailed planned Soviet programmes. There is no doubt that the deployment of Soviet ABM was halted below the planned level, though how far the Soviet Union would have gone in deploying that system remains unclear. In the case of land-based missiles, the *size* of the force was reduced from planned levels, since at the very least the Soviet Union was required to dismantle her SS-7s and SS-8s. But the modernization programme was probably no more than inconvenienced by the requirement to use or modify existing silos. Sea-based missile forces were probably kept somewhat below originally planned levels, but qualitatively they evidently proceeded as planned.

The basic thrust of offensive Soviet strategic force programmes has not been and will apparently not be affected by SALT II, but neither is it likely that the equivalent American programmes will be affected.

What seems to be motivating the Soviet Union principally in the SALT negotiations is the desire to block drastic advances by the United States, such as those initiated by the Kennedy Administration and, in the Soviet view, by the MIRV programmes of the late 1960s and early 1970s. It is for this reason that the Soviet Union has made such an issue of the cruise missile, for she sees in it a system that could pose major new problems for her defences and could undermine the 'equal-security' balance to which she believes herself entitled. It may well prove to have been one of the more serious Soviet miscalculations to have believed that the United States would leave unanswered the threat both to her fixed land-based missile launchers and to the penetrability of her manned bomber force.

The outcome of SALT II remains uncertain at the time of writing. But what can be said of the SALT process as a whole, as well as of the apparently unending Mutual and Balanced Force Reduction (MBFR) talks, is that the Soviet Union has not participated in them on the basis of abstract notions such as 'stable deterrence' or the halting of the 'arms spiral'. This kind of language is, of course, no longer foreign to the Soviet Union, and the old slogans about halting the arms race still abound in Soviet discourse. But the reality seems more sober and more limited. The dangers the Soviet Union sees lie not in an abstract arms race but in weapons programmes that could offset her own, in specific new systems that would pose specific threats and in some eventual reversal of the trends in the power balance, perhaps at a time when China will begin to become a serious strategic as well as a land power. The fundamental response of the Soviet Union to such threats remains what it has always been: to look to her own strength. But it is a mark of the Brezhnev era, foreshadowed tentatively by that of Khrushchev, that negotiations and agreements on arms limitation are seen as having a role to play in augmenting unilateral programmes by slowing the programmes of the other side – provided, of course, there are programmes on the other side worth paying a price to slow down.

CONCLUSION

The emerging situation for Soviet security policy in the next decade could resemble that of 1958–62, when Khrushchev attempted to turn a military advantage into lasting geo-political gains. But there would be a significant difference: Soviet military power would meanwhile have gone through some twenty years of modernization and enlargement. Strategic forces would be massive and diverse rather than rudimentary. Close to a generation of momentum in military growth would be behind the Soviet leadership of the day and by all indications this momentum would not be arrested, even if anticipated economic slowdown increased its relative cost.

Yet when all of this is added up, would Soviet leaders in the end dismiss the forces that would be arrayed against them in any open and direct challenge to the international geo-political balance? Would political leaders, including those principally charged with the development and modernization of the Soviet economy and with managing far-flung ties with the outside world, accept without serious reservation estimates that the gains to be derived from pressure, threats and, ultimately, the use of force, are inevitably destined to outweigh the costs? Would Soviet leaders, even assuming they believed themselves to have gained substantial military advantages, be certain of their ability to control the course of crises or war? How certain would Soviet leaders be that the gains they made through pressure or force would, in fact, enhance the security of the Soviet state and the progress of its political system?

None of these questions can be answered conclusively by drawing on the experience of the past. Nothing in that portion of Soviet discourse available to us sheds clear light on the answers. The Soviet attacks on Finland, Poland and Bessarabia in 1939–40 took place in the anticipation of fairly imminent attack, but with a green or amber light from the enemy-to-be who was then still an ally. The moves into Angola and Ethiopia seem to have been based on the calculation that the risks were modest, and therefore they do not give us much guidance for gauging Soviet reaction in situations in which risks may be judged to be more serious. On the other hand, Soviet actions in successive crises over Berlin, the Middle East and Cuba, in which assertiveness was followed by caution when risks became higher than apparently anticipated, do not provide clear answers either. All these crises occurred before the military balance had reached the state prevailing now or that which is expected to prevail in the next five to ten years.

We thus reach a point where speculation about Soviet behaviour must inevitably merge with expectations of American behaviour and that of other powers in the world. We do not see a Soviet leadership brimming with optimism about the prospects of the USSR in relation to the United States, the Western world generally, China and others. But nor do we see that leadership overcome with pessimism. Its economic and other plans project effort and sacrifice for years to come. Its external economic and other commitments are also essentially long-term. Its military plans seem to envisage further cycles of modernization and improvement.

How a new leadership will handle this inheritance we cannot say. But whatever departures from Lenin it adds to those sanctioned already by its predecessors, we tend to believe that it will continue to adhere to Lenin's adaptation of Clausewitz: 'war is the continuation of the policies of peace; and peace, the continuation of the policies of war'.[2] If we are right in that judgment, then the West has it in its power to help the Soviet Union remain true to the scripture in this one fateful instance, by making certain that no meaningful political gain and no security advantage can be obtained from resort to the threat or use of force.

NOTES

[1] See William Epstein, *The Last Chance* (New York: The Free Press, 1976), p. 11.

[2] V. I. Lenin, *Bourgeois Pacifism and Socialist Pacifism* (March 1919).

ADELPHI PAPERS

The following is a selection of those available. They may be ordered from the Institute at a current price of £1.00 ($2.50) per copy, post free by Accelerated Surface Post or Bulk Air Mail (to non-UK destinations).

Discount rates are available for bulk orders of 11 or more Adelphi Papers of the same title.